Dirty Rotten

VIKINGS

THREE CENTURIES OF LONGSHIPS, LOOTING, AND BAD BEHAVIOR

J. M. Sertori

Illustrated by Mauro Mazzara

Ticktock

An Hachette UK Company
www.hachette.co.uk

First published in the USA in 2014 by Ticktock,
an imprint of Octopus Publishing Group Ltd
Endeavour House
189 Shaftesbury Avenue
London
WC2H 8JY

www.octopusbooks.co.uk
www.octopusbooksusa.com
www.ticktockbooks.com

Distributed in the US by
Hachette Book Group USA
1290 Avenue of the Americas
4th and 5th Floors
New York, NY 10020

Distributed in Canada by
Canadian Manda Group
664 Annette Street
Toronto, Ontario, Canada M6S 2C8

ISBN 978-1-78325-209-1
Printed and bound in China

COMMISSIONING EDITOR: Anna Bowles
MANAGING EDITOR: Karen Rigden
DESIGNER: Ceri Hurst
ART DIRECTOR: Miranda Snow
PRODUCTION CONTROLLER: Sarah-Jayne Johnson

DIRTY ROTTEN VIKINGS PICTURE ACKNOWLEDGMENTS

akg-images 9. Alamy 19th era 42 below; Heritage Image Partnership Ltd 21; Interfoto 29 below right; Ivy Close Images
17; Jorge Royan 6 above; Mary Evans Picture Library 57 main; MCLA Collection 26; North Wind Picture Archives 12, 52
left; Scenics & Science 1. Fotolia TheStockCube 58 below. Freeimages 24 above, 25 left. Getty Images British Library/
Robana 40 left; De Agostini 36 below right; Dorling Kindersley 30; Heritage Images 54 below; Jeff J Mitchell 62 below
right; Leemage/Universal Images Group 33 above right; Peter V. Bianchi/National Geographic 51 below; Print Collector
5; Ted Spiegel/National Geographic 22 right; The LIFE Picture Collection 48 below; Walter Bibikow 22 left. Shutterstock
Claudine Van Massenhove 60 below right; Jan Miko 46 below; javarman 34 below; Stewart Smith Photography 39 center;
SurangaSL 18. Thinkstock cmfotoworks 45 right.

CONTENTS

THE FURY OF THE NORTHMEN

They came out of nowhere

They came out of nowhere.
On a wet June day in AD 793,
raiders fell upon the undefended monastery island of Lindisfarne off the northeast English coast. They murdered anyone who stood in their way, killed priests and monks, and dragged away children to make them become slaves.

A LIFE OF CRIME

The Vikings were men from Scandinavia who had turned to a life of crime, targeting coastal sites within sailing distance of their homeland. They may have taken their name from *vik*, meaning the bay where they kept their ships, but the word *Viking* soon came to mean a pirate, slaver, or criminal.

LIKE DUNG IN THE STREET

The Lindisfarne Stone is inscribed with images of raiders. "The pagans have ruined God's sanctuary," wrote the bishop Alcuin. "They shed the blood of martyrs around the altar, laid waste the house of our hope, and trampled the bodies of saints like dung in the street."

This carving from Lindisfarne was made after the Viking attack and commemorates the terrifying event.

SHOCK AND AWE

Lindisfarne was like a terrorist attack, leading Christians all over Europe to pray for safety from further raids. One prayer went: *"Save us, O God, by preserving our bodies and those in our care from the wild Norse people who ravage our realms."*

VIKING CRIME SCENE INVESTIGATION

Did the Vikings really come from nowhere?
Why did they suddenly attack Lindisfarne?

TRADERS TURN RAIDERS

Wicings ("traders," in the Anglo-Saxon language) had been sailing from Scandinavia to the British Isles for many years. Four years before the attack on Lindisfarne, a sheriff had been murdered in the southern town of Portland when he tried to tell three Norse trading ships they were not welcome.

HACKSILVER

Lindisfarne was a prime target because the monastery had many valuable items like candlesticks and silver bowls, and also religious donations. It was undefended, because nobody imagined anyone would attack a church in a Christian country. But Christian belief meant nothing to the thieves, who smashed up priceless objects to divide the spoils. These fragments formed a kind of money among the Vikings, known as hacksilver.

Viking jewelry and clothing clasps.

THREE'S A CROWD

Many early reports of Vikings mention just three ships. It is possible they were the same three ships each time, and that the first few years of Viking attacks were the work of a single gang. They probably didn't even go home to Norway, but lurked each winter somewhere in the Scottish isles.

STAY OFFA

Why didn't they go further south? The year before the Lindisfarne raid, King Offa of Mercia had built coastal defenses sufficient to keep pirates away. The first Vikings only picked easy targets.

FORGOTTEN SCOTLAND

Archeological evidence shows there were many other raids in northern Scotland and the northern isles, but nobody survived to tell the tale. Within ten years of Lindisfarne, part of north-west Scotland was a Viking kingdom called Laithlinn. Lindisfarne is remembered as the "first" raid, because it was the first time Vikings took on the Church. In the middle ages, it was monks who wrote the history!

THE NORSE CREATION MYTH

Mad as beans

The Vikings had their own religion, which was quite crazy and seemingly made up when they were drunk.

IN THE BEGINNING...

...there was nothing. Just a black void. And a river. And land for the river to flow on. And a sea for it to flow to. And a hill for it to flow down. But apart from that, *nothing*—do you hear? Oh, but there was ice.

UDDERLY DISGUSTING

The first creatures were Ymir (a giant) and Audhumbla (a cow), both born from the poisonous waters of an icy river. Ymir stayed alive by sucking on the cow's udders, while she licked a lump of salty ice until Buri, the first god, broke free.

PIT STOP

The first man and first woman were born from Ymir's armpits. No, it doesn't really bear thinking about.

MURDER ONE

Buri's grandchildren were three gods: Odin, Vili, and Ve. Because they were proper Vikings, they killed Ymir the giant and then used his corpse to make the world. His skull is the dome of the sky. The Earth is his body. His blood is the ocean. Trees are made from his hair and the clouds are his brain. You live on one of his eyebrows. We never said this would be easy.

Over the centuries people have drawn and painted the Norse creation myths. They have one thing in common: they're all weird!

THE WORLD TREE

Everything rests on the World Tree, Yggdrasil. The gods live in Asgard in its top branches. Hell and the worlds of giants and elves are scattered among its roots. We live in Midgard, the Middle World. Bifrost, the rainbow bridge, connects our world to the world of the gods.

9

SLABLAND
Nothing here
but rocks

GREENLAND
Not green at all.
They lied to us!

ICELAND
Volcanoes.
Cold farms. Shaggy ponies.

FORESTLAND
Nothing but trees.
Handy for boatbuilding.

VINLAND
People say there are grapes here.
Plus the chance to get murdered
by the natives.

BRITAIN
Gold and slaves.
Some farmland worth stealing.
Cabbages.

THE VIKING WORLD

Places to rob

The world of the Vikings stretched
from their Scandinavian homeland
as far south as the Mediterranean,
and as far west as America.

NORWAY
The "north way," scattered with little islands and inlets for boats.

THE KEEL Mountain range and rumored home of elves and giants..

FINLAND
Lakes.
o Furry animals.o

RUS LAND
Cousins have holed up here.
Plenty of fighting.
Rivers to the south.

SWEDEN
Where the Swedes come from.

LINDISFARNE
Unguarded treasure.

DENMARK
Land of the Danes.
Something is usually rotten here.

NORMANDY
Settled by Norsemen.

CONSTANTINOPLE
THE GREATEST CITY IN THE WORLD.
Always looking for Norsemen to work as guards.

ITIL
Sell slaves here.

GODS OF THE VIKINGS

Thunder and lightning

Originally there was no "family" of Viking gods,
just different idols worshiped in bits of Scandinavia.
Here are just some of them.

ODIN AND HIS OCTOHORSE

Because he was popular with Viking sailors, Odin was often thought of as the "leader" of the gods. He poked out one of his eyes in exchange for knowledge—not the smartest thing to do, but he did learn how to write things down in runes. He was advised by two ravens, Hugin and Munin, who would report to him about world news, and he rode on an eight-legged horse, Sleipnir. It's thought that this might have its origin in the legs of four pallbearers, carrying a corpse.

Odin gets some shut-eye—before he goes and pokes one of them out.

ONE-ARMED BANDIT

Tyr was the Norse god of war. His hand was bitten off by the giant wolf Fenrir. OK—not a particularly competent god of war, then.

HAMMER TIME!

Often shown with red hair and associated with fire, Thor is well known as the god of thunder. In ancient Scandinavia, the sound of thunder was said to be the rumbling of his chariot wheels. He carries the hammer Mjolnir, which can crush mountains. Thor's hammer was often worn as a pagan lucky charm, as opposed to the crucifix worn by medieval Christians.

HEIMDALL

Heimdall was the guardian of Bifrost, the rainbow bridge. He guarded against attacks by giants. In the case of an attack, he would blow on Gjallarhorn, his magical trumpet, to warn the other gods.

GODDESSES
OF THE VIKINGS

Scary women

There were just as many Norse goddesses as gods, although male Vikings tended not to pay attention to most of them.

DIDN'T SEE THAT COMING

Odin's wife, Frigg, had the power of prophecy, although she kept her knowledge to herself. She is most famous for loving her son Baldur so much that she got every beast and plant in the world to swear never to harm him. This made Baldur invulnerable to all weapons... except one. The trickster god Loki killed Baldur with a dart made out of mistletoe, which Frigg had forgotten (not so good at seeing the future after all, then).

CRONE WARS

Only one person ever defeated Thor in a wrestling match, and that was Elli, the super-strong giantess, who wrestled him to his knees. Elli was a symbol of old age, which overcomes everybody, given time.

The Norwegians still make sculptures of Frigg. This one marks the opening of an oil field in 1978.

LADY LOVE

Freya, goddess of love, rides in a chariot pulled by cats, or on a magical giant boar. She had many suitors. One of them, a giant, stole Thor's hammer and demanded Freya's hand in marriage as the price of returning it. Thor dressed up in Freya's wedding gown and fooled the giants, though they did smell a rat when the "bride" ate and drank like a horse. Thor grabbed his hammer and slaughtered them all.

LASTING FAME

Freya remained a powerful fertility goddess in Scandinavia long after the Viking age. Up until the 19th century, charms in her name could be seen in Sweden, placed in fields to bring good harvests.

LOKI

The worst of the Viking gods

If everybody was scared of the Vikings,
what were the Vikings scared of?
It was bad luck, in the form of Loki, the trickster
god who loved to make life difficult.

SHAPE-SHIFTER

Some sources say Loki was a very short giant, others that he was was a naughty god who loved playing tricks on people and trying out new insults on the other gods. He could change shape, causing mischief in the form of a bird, a fish, a horse, or even an old lady, as well as in his normal form.

HORRIBLE KIDS

Loki's children included Odin's horse Sleipnir; Hel; the Goddess of, well, Hell; Fenrir the horrible wolf that bit off the hand of the god of war, and Jormungand, the World Serpent that encircles the entire planet.

ON THE OTTER HAND...

Loki stole a magic ring from the dwarf Andvari, who cursed anyone who touched his treasure. When Loki killed an otter, it turned out to be a shape-shifting dwarf. Loki had to pay all his gold to the angry family, but when he used the ring to cover the last part of the debt, the curse was passed on to them, and all their descendants, creating a whole cycle of tragic deaths and misunderstandings. The story inspired Wagner's opera series *The Ring of the Nibelung,* as well as Tolkien's *Lord of the Rings.*

ONE IN THE EYE

As punishment for causing Baldur's death, Loki was tied up with a serpent dripping poison in his eyes. Loki's wife would try to catch it in a dish, but every time she turned away to empty it, he'd get another drip in the face. His agonized writhing caused earthquakes. He could only break free at the end of the world.

BRYNHILDR AND THE VALKYRIES

Choosers of the slain

The Valkyries were legendary warrior women who rode out onto battlefields to pick the best of the dead warriors to bring to Odin's home, Valhalla, the Viking heaven. There they fought, feasted, and drank. The party was set to continue until the day came when they would fight in Odin's last battle.

GHOST RIDERS

Vikings said that the sight of the Northern Lights in the night sky was the Valkyries riding out in search of new recruits. They had no other explanation for the crazy light show of shimmering colors, which is actually caused by wind from the sun hitting charged particles in the Earth's atmosphere.

WHAT A PRETTY NAME...

Valkyries were the Viking man's idea of perfect women—bold, beautiful, and battle-crazy.

Their names include
Geirdriful (Spear Flinger), *Göndul* (Wand Wielder), *Herja* (Devastator), *Skalmöld* (Sword Time), and *Svipul* (Unstable).

BRIGHT BATTLE

Brynhildr, "Bright Battle," was the most famous of the Valkyries, banished to Earth as a mortal woman after she favored someone in a fighting match against Odin's wishes. She slept beneath a wall of shields and a ring of fire until she was rescued by the hero Sigurd.

THE FAT LADY SINGS

Brynhildr was the inspiration for the character of Brünnhilde in Richard Wagner's opera *The Valkyrie*. In this version, she is rescued by the hero Siegfried, but he forgets her when he drinks a magic potion. In the opera *Twilight of the Gods* (even operas have sequels) she kills herself (after a long song) by throwing herself onto Siegfried's funeral pyre, signaling the beginning of the end of the world. It is from this that we get the phrase "It ain't over till the fat lady sings."

HARALD FAIRHAIR

Bad hair day

The first true king of Norway was Harald Fairhair (850–932), who got his name when he promised his girlfriend he would not cut his hair or marry her until he had conquered the whole land. Ten years later, his head was a tangled, greasy mess of knots. Some called him Tanglehair, but it's best not to be too insulting to a man with his own army, so "Fairhair" stuck.

MR. UNPOPULAR

Although he brought peace to Norway, Harald brought disaster to many other countries, as enemies fled his unpopular taxes and laws and turned to robbery abroad. His reign led to increased Viking attacks on Britain, Ireland, and the rest of Europe, as well as the large-scale settlement of Iceland.

This Norse manuscript shows Harald cutting bonds from the giant Dofri, who was his foster father according to folklore.

WHO'S YOUR DADDY?

Most Viking surnames simply announced who your father was: like Eriksen, Olafson, Sigurdsdottir, or Magnusdottir. Very rarely, someone with a fearsome mother would use her name instead, such as Svein Estridsen, whose mother was a queen. Other surnames were based on nicknames, and usually showed how tough you were by what your friends could get away with.

PICK A VIKING NAME

(all these are real):

YOUR FIRST NAME
+
ONE OF THESE:

Bloodax

The Boneless

The Careless

The Deep-minded

The Evil

Fairhair

Fart

The Fat

Hairy Pants

Half Troll

Hog Head

Hump

The Lame

Long Legs

Redbeard

Rednose

The Sarcastic

The Shifty

Skull-splitter

Spike

The Unwashed

The Victorious

THE VIKING SHIP

Here be dragons

The most infamous kind of Viking ship was the "Dragon" longship. These fast, narrow ships were designed for attack. Sadly, archaeologists have never found one, as they tended to get smashed up, or burned in Viking funerals.

DRAGON HEADS

These were sometimes removable—just in case the Vikings were visiting friendly towns and didn't want to bring them bad luck.

Bucket and Chuck It

LONGSHIPS WERE OPEN TO THE ELEMENTS. LUXURIES INCLUDED:

- **FOOD:** *Eaten raw or cooked on a dangerous open-air barbecue*

- **SEATING:** *Rowers sat on storage chests*

- **BEDS:** *Forget it: you slept on the deck*

- **TOILETS:** *Forget those too: you did it overboard and drip-dried*

BEACH IT

Many Viking ships were light enough to be carried by their crews, allowing them to be carried short distances between lakes and rivers. This made the Vikings much more mobile, able to travel much farther inland than their victims expected.

ONBOARD

Longboat sails were made of wool, and probably smelled like a wet dog once they got damp. The rudder or "steer-board" was usually placed on the right-hand side. The rudder was kept on the far side from a harbor dock in order not to damage it. This is the origin of our modern nautical terms "PORT" (left) and "STARBOARD" (right). Shields were stored along the sides and added extra protection.

NAVIGATION

Vikings steered by the stars, or used a primitive sundial to work out where they were. They also kept an eye out for clouds or flocks of birds, both likely to form close to land, even if the land had not yet come into sight.

THE RUS

Vikings accidentally invent Russia

Not all Vikings sailed on the sea.
Several groups used rivers, too, grabbing island
strongholds and hefting their ships across
waterfalls, rapids, and between lakes.

KING BY INVITATION

According to Eastern European legend, quarreling
local tribes invited Viking warriors to come and
rule over them. This seems too good to be true,
but some still believe that the Swedish leader
Rurik and his two brothers were the first of the
"Rus"—a bunch of Vikings who spread along the
Don and Volga river systems.

NAME CHANGES...

The Rus stuck to islands and demanded
protection money from people in the
surrounding area. They were mainly men
and took local wives, so that within a
few generations, their children were not
"Scandinavian" any more. Some names
still persisted in mangled form, like Ingvar
(as Igor) and Helga (as Olga). The center
of their power was around Kiev, in what
is now Ukraine.

*This 19th-century
Russian painting
shows the Vikings
turning up in what
was to become Rus.*

GREEK FIRE

They attacked Constantinople in the south, but were beaten back by medieval flamethrowers—the infamous Greek fire. Instead, they started trading with the Greek world, buying silk and other luxuries with fur and amber.

WHAT'S A RUS?

Rhos—Greek for rosy-skinned?

Rods—Old Swedish for a rower?

Rusioi—Greek for blonds?

Whatever the word originally meant, descendants of the Rus were known as *Rusici* among themselves, and *Russiya* among the Arabs. Their homeland eventually came to be known as Russia.

SLAVERS AND TRADERS

Sale now on

The Rus traveled through the river systems of Eastern Europe, all the way to the Black Sea and Caspian Sea. At Itil, at the mouth of the Volga River, they sold their cargo to slavers from the Muslim world. Muslim writers got to see the Vikings up close, not as enemies but as fellow merchants.

PIECES OF SILVER

The *dirham*, a coin from the Muslim world, was valued by the Vikings for its silver content. Many thousands of them have been found in Viking graves all over Scandinavia. That suggests that traders kidnapped people from the coasts, dragged them to the south and sold them.

BODY ART

Muslim observers noted that the Vikings were heavily tattooed all over their bodies, and that the men even wore eyeliner. Ahmad ibn Fadlan met Rus traders at Itil and said he had "never seen more perfect physical specimens, as tall as palm trees, blond and ruddy."

WASH AND BLOW

Ahmad ibn Fadlan was less impressed with their hygiene. He watched the Vikings in the morning pass around a bowl of water to wash their faces, each of them finishing up by blowing snot into the bowl, spitting in it, and passing it on. Imagine being the last in line!

THINGS I HATE ABOUT THE VIKINGS

By Ahmad ibn Fadlan

- They don't wash after eating.
- They poop in public.
- They are as stupid as donkeys.

WALKING BANKS

Ahmad ibn Fadlan also noted that the Rus would store their wealth by buying expensive necklaces for their wives, decorated with amber, glass beads, and coins. Well, they didn't have wallets, or pockets to put them in.

GOING BERSERK

You won't like him when he's angry

The early Vikings were criminal gangs who placed great value on the best fighters, even though that often meant some were incredibly dangerous psychopaths. If someone was so tough that he even scared the Vikings, they persuaded him to be the first off the boat and into battle. That way, he'd be someone else's problem.

WOLF-MEN

Some Vikings fought without armor, wearing wolfskins or bearskins. These fighters became so mad with rage that they were unstoppable. They would chew on their shields or possibly take drugs to become battle-crazed. They were known as *ulfhednar* (wolfskins) or *berserkers* (bear-shirts). Stories about them might explain some European legends about werewolves.

A Viking-era bronze plate showing Odin and a beserker with the head of a wolf.

MAD KILLERS

Berserkers were the toughest and most frightening of the Vikings, but also the most stupid—who else would volunteer to charge into battle unprotected? (Later, in the Middle Ages, "berserk" came to be used in Iceland to refer to criminals and thugs.) When the raiding days were over, maddened killers were less welcome in polite society.

"They rushed forward without armor, were as mad as dogs or wolves, bit their shields, and were strong as bears or wild oxen, and killed people at a blow, but neither fire nor iron told upon them. This was called Berserkergang."—Ynglinga Saga.

Berserkers were so well known in Viking society that they even showed up in games, like this chess piece chewing on his shield.

MR AND MRS BLOODAX

Love at first smite

Eric Bloodax and his wife Gunnhild Kingsmother were the celebrity couple of the Viking era. He was a murderous pirate and she was a witch.

KINSLAYER

Son of Harald Fairhair, Eric was described by the sagas as tall and handsome, but "violent of disposition." He killed his first man aged 12, and became a pirate soon after. You can guess why he was called Bloodax. He got the extra nickname of Kinslayer when he killed several of his brothers.

MOTHER OF KINGS

Erik met Gunnhild Kingsmother in Finland, where she had been learning sorcery from local Saami shamans. The sagas say she was the most beautiful woman anyone had ever seen, and that she could transform into a bird.

EXILES

Pushed out of Scandinavia by rivals, the couple moved to the British Isles, where they made their living by robbing and murdering. They spent much of their lives in exile, but several of their children became kings of Norway.

NAG, NAG, NAG

Erik got into a long feud with a poet called Egil. Egil killed one of Erik's sons and put a curse on Mr. and Mrs. Bloodax with a "spite-post." This turned out to be a real horse's head on a stick, pointed to stare threateningly at Erik's homeland, and carved with rude insults.

SINGALONGA BLOODAx

According to the sagas, Gunnhild fought back by casting a spell on Egil that made him feel depressed. Eventually, however, Egil was captured by Erik and won him over by composing a song about him. This apparently made everything all right, although Gunnhild sulked a bit at first.

A STICKY END

Eric was killed around 952 while fighting in the north of England. After Erik's death, Gunnhild's power dwindled. She was eventually drowned in a Danish bog by orders of a rival king around 977.

ANTI-VIKING MEASURES

How to stop a floating drive-by

The people of Europe came up with several methods of resisting the Vikings. These included watchmen to monitor the coast for them, warriors to fight them, and bribes to make them go away. The only ways to beat a Viking were to kill him, or give him so much cash that he couldn't carry any more.

A BRIDGE TOO FAR?

With Paris under Viking attack, the French fortified the bridges across the Seine. The fighting went on for two months, until the Vikings escaped upriver. The French let them go, because Burgundy was upriver and nobody liked the Burgundians. When the Vikings came back after robbing Burgundy, the French king paid them in silver to go away.

FRENCH LEAVE

The French met their match in the form of Hrolf Ganger (Rollo the Walker), a giant Norwegian Viking who fled the reforms of Harald Fairhair and attacked the French coast. He was so successful that the French gave up and simply gave the region to him, making him the first duke of the land of the Northmen, or *Normandy*. This was great if you were a Viking and not such good news if you were English, because now there was an entire Viking kingdom on the other side of the English Channel.

PAYBACK

The Saxon poem "The Battle of Maldon" celebrates Brythnoth, a Saxon general who led a squad of men to resist a Viking landing at Maldon in 991. The Viking leader, Olaf Crowbone, offered to leave if they paid him in "gold and armor." Brythnoth replied: "We will pay you with spear tips and sword blades." But Brythnoth and his men were killed.

EVERYBODY'S GONE TO ICELAND

Even further north

Viking sailors in the 800s found
a large island far to the northwest.
It had thin, dark soil, fiery volcanoes, and towering glaciers.
The winters were cold, but in summer it was "light enough
to pick the lice from your clothes." Heavenly.

NOT REALLY FIRST

Although the Vikings claimed to have "discovered" Iceland, it's likely that it already was home to a small population of Irish and Scottish hermits and monks, who were looking for somewhere peaceful to live. No luck there...

NOT REALLY VIKINGS

Despite its unappealing name, Iceland was soon settled by Vikings who wanted to become farmers. One of the first settlers was Ingolf, who was on the run for murder. Although the settlers of Iceland were from Scandinavia, many brought slaves kidnapped from the coasts of Ireland. These people made up a quarter of the first settlers. Many later Icelanders would have Irish-sounding names like Bran or Patrek.

LOCAL CUISINE

Because Icelandic shark meat is poisonous, the only way to prepare it was to bury it in a sandpit under some rocks and to let it rot for a few months. The resulting "hakarl" smells like, well, rotting shark and tastes like, well, rotting shark. Really. How did someone discover this recipe?

LINKS TO THE PAST

Cut off from Europe, Iceland became a treasure house of Viking knowledge. The language remains very similar to Old Norse, and the long winter nights led to the preservation of many Viking stories. Much of what we know about the Vikings has come to us through their descendants in Iceland.

Picking lice from your clothes—an important Viking skill.

THE GREAT HEATHEN HOST

No more smash and grab

By the late 9th century Vikings were not just scattered raiding parties but massive armies. Some stole and ran, but others planned on seizing something they couldn't take away with them—the land itself.

GREAT EXPECTATIONS

The Viking leader Guthrum fought a long series of battles with the Wessex king, Alfred. Remembered today as "Alfred the Great," Alfred bribed the Vikings to go away, and when that failed, let them stay as long as Guthrum converted to Christianity. He must have hoped that changing religions would turn the Vikings into nice people. Good luck with that.

King Alfred the Great

THAT FANCY LONDON

Alfred fortified the easternmost bridging point of the Thames River, which led deep into his homeland of Wessex. This led him to occupy and rebuild the old ruins of Londinium, a Roman city now called London.

THE DANELAW

Because of Alfred's treaty with Guthrum, England was split, with much of the east now a Viking kingdom— the Danelaw. Although this was soon incorporated back into England, Scandinavian customs, law, and language would endure there for hundreds of years.

THERE GOES THE NEIGHBORHOOD

Although Alfred had to give away half the country, he gave away the half that was most likely to be attacked by Vikings. Just like the French in Normandy, he had solved his Viking problem by forcing them to put up with the next wave of attacks themselves. The new Viking area was called the Danelaw, because "Danes" were in charge there.

Britain in the late 9th century

NORTHUMBERLAND

THE DANELAW

DANISH MERCIA

ENGLISH MERCIA

WALES

WESSEX AND ITS DEPENDENCIES

VIKING WORDS

Who knew?

Many words in modern English were brought into the language by the "Danes" who lived in the Danelaw, such as *snubba* (curse; now used as snub), or *steik* (fry; now used as steak). *Slahtr* meant to butcher animals, and is the origin of our word "slaughter."

ANIMAL FARM

Myca came out of the back end of a cow, and is the origin of our word "muck." If it came out of a human, it was called *drit*, which stays with us as "dirt." Vikings would go fishing by putting *beita* on the end of their fishhooks. A baby goose was a *goesling*. An egg was... an *egg*.

KNOW YOUR PLACE

Other Viking words survive in place names, like Dublin (*dubh linn*—the "black pool") or Wexford (*veisafjord*—"bay by the mudflats"). Many place names, particularly in the British Isles or places settled by the British, have Viking elements, such as Grimsby or Westham.

Viking Place Names

Berg—Hill

By—Homestead

Dale—Valley

Feld—Field

Ham—Village

Holm—Island

Ton—Town

Thorpe—Farm

Thwaite—Meadow

Wick—Bay

A thousand years ago, Britain was a rolling landscape of bergs, dales, felds, and thwaites.

WEDDING DAZE

If a Norse woman wanted to get married, she would invite *gestr* to her home. The master of the house would be known as her *husbondi*. Her parents would dress her up nicely so that she would *glitra* with gold and didn't look *uggligr*. This was her dowry, or in Norse, her *gift*. If they couldn't find something, they would have to *rannsaka* (search the house) for it. If they still couldn't find it, they must be *blundra* (with one eye shut).

THE ST BRICE'S DAY MASSACRE

Kill them all!

Just because the Danes lived more peacefully among the English, it didn't make the resentment go away. There were still Viking raids, and King Aethelred had to pay bribes to the Danish king, Sweyn Forkbeard, to stay away.

BAD COMPANY

Aethelred is remembered as "the unready," although his nickname was really *Unraed*, which means "the badly advised." Told that there was a Danish plot to murder him, he ordered the deaths of every Dane in England. The killings began on November 13, 1002, which was St. Brice's Day.

SEEKING SANCTUARY

One group of Danes tried to barricade themselves in a church. The mob chasing them set fire to the building, not only killing the occupants, but burning the Christian relics, Bibles, and everything else inside. Archaeologists have found several mass graves dating from the time, piled with skeletons. Most are wounded on the back of the head, suggesting they were running away when they were struck.

DANE DOORS

Legends grew up, particularly in Essex in the east of England, that the thick leather coverings of certain church doors were made from the skins of murdered Danes. However, for this to be true, the skins would have had to come from very big Danes, roughly the size and shape of cows. Modern DNA testing has so far confirmed that they're just normal leather.

FORKBEARD

One of the murdered Danes was Sweyn Forkbeard's sister. Even if he hadn't planned on attacking England, now he had an excuse. He invaded with an army, chased Aethelred out of the country, and proclaimed himself king. He died five weeks later, leaving England in the hands of his son, Cnut.

CNUT THE GREAT

Life's a beach

Cnut the Great (aka King Canute) inherited Denmark and England from his Viking father Sweyn Forkbeard, becoming the ruler of a short-lived empire that spanned the North Sea.

SHAME ABOUT THE NOSE

Cnut was described as a tall and handsome man "except for his nose, which was thin, high, and hooked." His conquest of England and successful reign almost turned Britain into a Scandinavian province, although none of his sons lived long enough to keep hold of it.

ZOO LANDERS

He landed in England in 1015 with 10,000 men in 200 longships, and fought a year-long war against the English king, Edmund Ironside. An overly poetic bard described his ships as containing "lions and bulls, their horns shining gold." He actually meant there were tough *men* onboard carrying swords and spears, but it's one of the misunderstandings that has led to pictures of Vikings with horned helmets.

Edmund Ironside (left) and Canute (right) shake hands. The friendliness didn't last

TURNING THE TIDE

Cnut ruled England for 19 years, and is remembered as a wise and successful king, partly because his Scandinavian contacts ended most Viking attacks during the period. He is most famous for a legend about his annoyance with flatterers at his court who boasted that he was so powerful he could command the seas. To prove he was just a man, Cnut had his throne put on the beach, where he made a point of ordering the sea around and failing to turn the tide.

That story was first written down 200 years after Cnut's death, which makes it very likely that someone made the whole thing up.

OLAF THE STOUT

Because it's rude to say "fat"

Olaf the Stout (995–1030), also known as Olaf the Fat and later as *Saint* Olaf (no, really), was a descendant of Harald Fairhair, who successfully reunited the scattered mini-kingdoms of Norway.

LONDON BRIDGE
IS FALLING DOWN

Olaf was one of a group of Vikings who attacked London in 1014, and used the power of their oarsmen to pull down the fortified bridge that blocked their passage up the river. Using longships without masts, protected by wet wooden roofs, he rowed close to the bridge, tied ropes to its supports, and then pulled it down by rowing hard downstream.

A GAME OF THRONES

Olaf was the ruler of Norway for only a brief time before he was kicked out by rivals who favored the claim of Cnut the Great. Olaf's big chance came at the Battle of Stiklastad, where he prayed the Christian God would bring him a suitable fate. He led his men in a fierce charge, hoping to scare as many of his enemies as possible before they realized how small his army really was.

The Norwegian flag with Olaf's coat of arms

THE **LION KING**

Olaf was killed at Stiklastad, but one of his killers reported that touching Olaf's blood had healed his own wounds. His friend, the English bishop Grimkell, soon proclaimed that other miracles had occurred in Olaf's name. Olaf was referred to as "Norway's eternal king" and he eventually became the country's patron saint. To this day, the lion in the Norwegian coat of arms carries Olaf's ax. Olaf's holy day is July 29.

UNRELIABLE CHRISTIANS

During the 11th century, many of the Viking lands converted to Christianity, the very religion whose believers many of them had been preying upon. But it was often a political decision, and a conversion that was forced on the local people.

BE NICE, OR ELSE!

Many Viking leaders became Christians because they wanted to be part of the sophisticated European world. Olaf Crowbone and Olaf the Stout both ordered everyone they met to become Christian and accept the love of Christ, or else they would burn down their houses and kill their families. Once a church was in the town center, locals got used to it and began to accept it.

ROUND ONE!

Some converts were very zealous. Thangbrand the missionary killed several pagans in Iceland who refused to believe in the Christian God. He met his match in Steinunn, a feisty old lady who said that Thor had challenged Christ to a fight, but Christ had never shown up.

Viking church in Lom, Norway

HEDGING YOUR BETS

Christianity for many was a new fashion trend. Some blacksmiths hedged their bets by continuing to make Thor's Hammer amulets alongside Christian crucifixes.

STOP HORSING AROUND

Several popes complained about the free and easy Christianity being practiced in former Viking areas. They suspected, rightly, that people in Iceland were still worshiping the old gods in secret. Excavations in some old churches have even found evidence of animal sacrifices, with horses buried in the foundations, and Norse gods hidden among the carvings. Elements of Yule, the Norse midwinter celebration, persist in Christmas traditions.

Christians don't put possessions in their graves, which means that the archaeological record from grave goods sharply declines in the late Middle Ages.

ERIK THE RED

Would you buy a farm from this man?

Red by name, red-hot-angry by nature,
the ginger-haired Erik Thorvaldson
grew up in exile in Iceland after his dad accidentally killed
someone. As an adult, Erik murdered his neighbor after
he refused to return some carved wooden beams that Erik
wanted out of the way while he renovated his house.

GO WEST!

Because Erik *might* have been provoked into killing his neighbor (and his neighbor's sons, and several people who tried to break up the fight), he got off lightly with a three-year exile. He chose to head west, to the remote rocks known as Gunnbjorn's Skerries, spotted by a lost Viking a few years earlier. Erik and his men discovered that the skerries were close to a much larger island, the western side of which had land suitable for farming.

This engraving shows Erik reaching Greenland

THE BIG LIE

Erik returned to Iceland full of stories about his discovery, and lured several thousand settlers to follow him to his new home. Because he wanted to make it sound like an attractive place, he decided to call it Greenland, even though it was icier than Iceland.

COME TO SUNNY GREENLAND

THERE'S LOADS OF FARMLAND.

IT'S NOT COLD AT ALL!

IF ANYONE SAYS IT'S COLD, WE WILL KILL THEM FOR YOU.

THE STRUGGLE FOR LIFE

Greenland was nowhere near as welcoming as Erik made it sound, but for many settlers, it was too late. They struggled to make ends meet in the two meager farming areas. Others headed north to hunt seals and walruses, where they fought with fur-clad natives we now know to be Inuit.

DESERTED

The settlements in Greenland held for several hundred years, although the settlers lost contact with Scandinavia in the 15th century. Later explorers found the villages ruined and burned.

LEIF ERIKSON

Go west, young man

Erik the Red's son was known as Leif the Lucky. He was famous for sailing directly to Norway from Greenland, through the open sea, in the hope that he would eventually hit something familiar. He reached Norway and became a Christian, sailing back home to convert his fellow Greenlanders.

VINLAND

Around AD 1000, Leif took his ships even farther west than Greenland, finding a barren land, then a forested land, and then an attractive countryside. His foster father Tyrkir claimed to have found grapes suitable for making wine, so Leif called it Vinland.

LEIF'S BOOTHS

Leif briefly settled on an island near the coast of his Vinland, and returned to Iceland the following year with a ship full of lumber and berries (probably not grapes after all). The site of his camp, "Leif's Booths," is thought to be in L'Anse aux Meadows, in what is now Newfoundland. Several later expeditions from Iceland would stay there over the next decade or so. A modern museum recreates life for Leif's crew.

YOUNG AMERICAN

Leif became a popular subject for American artists and sculptors in the 19th century, particularly as Scandinavian immigrants swelled the modern population. There may have been other Norse settlers, but Leif is the only one who is "Lucky" enough to have been both remembered in sagas and supported by archaeological evidence.

Viking settlers in North America

FREYDIS

She's a devil woman

Several members of Leif's family returned to his "booths" in Vinland in later years. Things went quite well until his sister Freydis turned up, as she was extremely volatile.

INDIAN GIVERS

Freydis probably first saw Vinland on the expedition of Thorfinn Karlsefni, where the travelers bought furs by trading red cloth and milk with the locals, who they called Skraelings (Screechers). Things turned bad when a Skraeling tried to take a weapon and got murdered. The exchange may not have been good for those who got away either—the Native Americans were probably lactose intolerant, meaning milk would give them stomach cramps and diarrhea.

TEMPER TIME

Freydis inherited the violent temper of her father, Erik the Red. When the explorers were attacked by Native Americans, Freydis called the Vikings cowards for running away. Pregnant and alone in the forest, she faced the attackers herself, topless and smacking her chest with a sword. They were so terrified of her that they ran away.

Note the horned helmet lurking in the bottom left of this rather overdramatic 19th-century painting of Freydis.

JUST A FEW MURDERS...

On her own expedition, she got into several fights with other Vikings about who could use the family camp. She eventually sent her men to kill her business partners while they slept, but nobody would kill five female witnesses. Freydis picked up an ax and killed them herself.

THE TRUTH COMES OUT...

She made the others promise not to tell of the murders. When they went back to Greenland, they claimed the missing people had decided to stay in Vinland. Eventually someone told Leif Erikson, but he could not bring himself to punish his sister. Instead, he cursed her and her descendants. After that, say the sagas of the Icelanders, "no one expected anything but evil from them."

THE VARANGIAN GUARD

Bodyguards with a difference

Some Vikings went all the way to Miklagard (the Great City), their name for Constantinople, where they worked as bodyguards of the Byzantine emperor. The rulers of Constantinople were so afraid of intrigues that they preferred to have foreign guards, and the giant, blond Scandinavians did the job.

PLEDGE OF ALLEGIANCE

Called "Varangians" (Pledgers) the Scandinavian soldiers fought as mercenaries in the Byzantine Empire's wars, traveling as far as the Holy Land, Sicily, and the coast of Africa. They favored shields and massive axes, and were the cause of many complaints about their loud off-duty boozing.

PILLAGE AWAY!

The Varangians had an odd right: that of being able to take as much gold as they could carry from the treasury of a dead emperor. This made many of them rich when they returned home to Scandinavia. Some were buried with Greek gold, or with Byzantine crosses on their tombs. The Varangians were loyal to whoever was emperor. Famously, when one emperor was killed, they simply served his successor, even if he was the man who killed him.

A 20th-century interpretation of the Varangians

HALFDAN WAS HERE

The Varangians had a rough reputation. One of them even carved his name in a balcony in the cathedral of Hagia Sophia, clearly bored during a long church service.

THE ENGLISH INVASION

The number of Scandinavians in the Varangian Guard declined after 1066, when their ranks were swelled by English refugees fleeing the Norman Conquest.

HARALD THE RUTHLESS

It's not a dress, it's armor

The last great Viking was Harald the Ruthless, who began his career as a teenage boy on the run, after the death of his half brother Olaf the Stout at the Battle of Stiklastad. He somehow made it out of Norway to the lands of the Rus, where he became a warrior in the retinue of Yaroslav the Wise.

WOMAN TROUBLE

Yaroslav's daughter Ellisif wasn't interested in Harald unless he had more money, so he went to Constantinople to become a Varangian Guard. He made a fortune fighting in Byzantine wars, although he was not particularly loyal to Emperor Michael IV—Harald poked out Michael's eyes. He had to leave in a hurry when the Empress Zoe took a shine to him and wanted him for herself.

SHARP-DRESSED MAN

After a long series of battles, Harald became the king of Norway and Denmark. He had a massive battleship called *The Serpent*, and a coat of chain mail so long that his men thought it was a dress and sometimes called him "Emma" as a joke.

1066 AND ALL THAT

Harald invaded England in 1066, but was killed in the Battle of Stamford Bridge. Although the English were victorious, they were so tired out by the effort that they weren't really ready for a second attack by William the Bastard from Normandy, who soon changed his name to William the Conqueror.

The Battle of Stamford Bridge

TWILIGHT
OF THE GODS

The Viking Apocalypse

The Vikings believed that the world would end in a massive war between gods and monsters, which they called *Ragnarok*. The last battle would pit Odin, his fellow gods, the Valkyries, and reborn Viking heroes, against an army of giants, serpents, and wolves, along with the bad god Loki.

WINTER IS COMING

Sagas and poems spoke of a terrible, long-lasting winter that would lead to conflicts and starvation. "Brother would fight brother," and there would be a time of swords, and a time of wolves. The sun would turn dark, and the World Serpent would move, causing earthquakes.

THE LAST STAND

The Viking gods and their enemies are so evenly matched that most of them fight to a lethal standstill. Odin is eaten by the wolf Fenrir, although his son Vidar rips the beast's jaws apart and stabs it in the heart. Thor kills the World Serpent, but staggers, poisoned, for only nine steps before he too collapses. At the end, almost everybody dies... but a new sun rises, and a lone man and woman inherit the Earth.

REAL-WORLD INSPIRATIONS

Parts of the Ragnarok story seem inspired by life on Iceland, particularly the fiery volcanoes and the colder climate of the 13th century, when the sagas were written down. Others might be inspired by Christianity, as a new order wipes away the traditions of olden times, bringing a new God, new heroes, and new people.

JERUSALEM-FARERS

What happened to the Vikings?

But Ragnarok never happened, so where did the Vikings actually go? Stories about them mainly disappear because after they became Christians, they stopped attacking churches and murdering monks. Christianity united them with the peoples they had formerly been robbing. So they all went off together and robbed someone else.

CRUSADERS

The Viking spirit lived on in the Jerusalem-farers—Scandinavian soldiers who joined up in the medieval Crusades and went to fight in the Holy Land. Crusades were also fought in Europe against the last pagans—in Finland, the Baltic countries, and the south of France, leading to the odd sight of Christian soldiers like Bishop Absalon from Denmark riding a horse and swinging an ax.

HARDAX WAS HERE

At Maeshowe in the Orkney Islands, a bunch of Jerusalem-farers broke into an old tomb in the 1150s to have a party. They also carved graffiti into the walls, announcing their names, including Ofram, Haermund Hardax, Ottarfila, and Benedikt, who carved a cross. In other news, apparently "Ingigerth is the most beautiful of all women." According to their graffiti, they came looking for treasure but didn't find any.

FADING AWAY?

Viking influence endured longer in remote places like Iceland and the Scottish islands. One king of Norway got the name Magnus Barelegs because he loved wearing kilts. The rest of the Vikings faded into history. Give a Viking a farm, and he's a farmer. Give him a foreign wife, and his children grow up speaking French, or English, or German. Make him a Christian, and he no longer worships Odin or steals from churches, so people stop calling him a Viking.

RELICS OF THE VIKINGS

Shadows of the Norsemen

There are still many relics of the Vikings in our modern world.

SANTA ODIN?

As an old bearded man from a snowy land, who pays attention to whether you have been naughty or nice, the god Odin might have inspired certain stories about Santa Claus. Santa doesn't demand human sacrifices, though, as far as we know.

UP-HELLY-AA

Some Viking traditions endure in places they settled, such as the torchlight Up-Helly-Aa procession in the Shetland Islands, where every year a massive longboat is given a fiery Viking funeral. The tradition only dates to the 1880s, but evokes Viking roots.

ANOTHER DAY, ANOTHER VIKING GOD

Several Viking gods have lent their names to the days of the week: Tyrsday (Tuesday), Odinsday (Wednesday), and Thorsday (Thursday). Friday is named either for Odin's wife, Frigg, or the Norse fertility goddess Freya—people are still arguing about it.

THE RED PLANET

In celebration of the Norse sailors' legendary ability to discover new lands, two NASA space probes sent to explore Mars in the 1970s were named Viking 1 and Viking 2.

09847007348   POLAROID032

The Viking 2 lander in orbit

THE MIGHTY THOR

The god Thor gained a newfound set of followers as the hero of his own comic book, in which he fought alongside other Marvel superheroes.

GLOSSARY

Allegiance: loyalty or devotion to some person, group, or cause, usually to a person in authority

Barren: incapable of producing offspring or growing things like food and plants

Barricade: a defensive barrier

Boar: a large wild pig with big tusks

Conversion: a change from one religion, belief, or political viewpoint to another

Corpse: a dead body, usually a human one

Descendants: people who are the children, grandchildren etc. of a specific person

Excavation: digging a hole to expose or unearth something

Fertility: the ability to produce offspring

Fortify: to protect or strengthen against attack

Heathen: someone who doesn't believe in the God of the Bible, so is neither a Christian, Jew, nor Muslim

Idol: image of a divine being other than the God of the Bible

Invulnerable: unable to be wounded, hurt, or damaged

Lure: to attract or tempt, often in a deceitful way

Monastery: a place where a community of monks lives

Pagan: someone who follows a religion with many gods, such as the ancient Romans or Greeks. The word can also mean "heathen"

Psychopath: someone who does violent things without feeling guilty. In modern medicine, they are considered to suffer from a personality disorder

Relics: objects that are traces of, or fragments from, the past

Renovate: to repair or return to a good condition, as if new

Ruse: a trick

Saga: a piece of medieval Icelandic or Norse prose